A Yeti Brew (And Bigfoot Too)

Mr. Satanism

Published by Inept Concepts, 2017.

While every precaution has been taken in the preparation of this book, the publisher assumes no responsibility for errors or omissions, or for damages resulting from the use of the information contained herein.

A YETI BREW (AND BIGFOOT TOO)

First edition. November 7, 2017.

ISBN: 979-8224876877

Written by Mr. Satanism.

Introduction

You know how sometimes someone super famous (like, say, Miley Cyrus, or Santa Claus) will be described as "needing no introduction"? Well that's how I feel about this book. It's a book about Bigfoot and Yeti movies; what part of that needs additional clarification? Sure, I could hold your hand and gently ease you into it, but if you ask me that seems kind of patronizing. It's not like you thought this was a cookbook or the latest intellectual trainwreck from Dean R. Koontz and are going to be all confused. Trust me, you can safely ignore this entire paragraph and get right down to business. That said, if you just plan on skimming the titles for viewing suggestions, all you really need to know is that the Abominable Snowman/Yeti movies are generally marginally better than the Sasquatch/Bigfoot movies. It's a surprisingly consistent distinction I'm at a total loss to explain.

Abominable

(2006)

Directed by Ryan Schifrin

The Mr. Satanism Movie Title Acid Test clearly states that you should never give your project a title that will make it (even) easier for movie critics to make fun of it, because those lazy shits will *always* go for the obvious diss. But I'll make an exception in this case, because let's face it, the Abominable Snowman *owns* the word *abominable.* I mean, besides him and Dr. Phibes, have you ever heard anyone or anything else regularly described as abominable? If you have, you're clearly hanging out with your opinionated grandmother too much. Of course it's all beside the point in this case, since this movie is clearly about a *Bigfoot,* not an Abominable Snowman. (Bigfoot is always brown, the Abominable Snowman is always white. If you want to turn this into a race thing that's your prerogative, but facts are facts.) Anyway, at first this looks like it's gonna be about an Abominable Bigfoot trapping a wheelchair-bound guy alone in an isolated cabin, which I suppose isn't the worst setup for a movie I've ever seen. I'll be honest though, I definitely perked up when the bachelorette party arrived and set up camp in the cabin next door. Bigfoot quickly grabs one of these chicks right in front of wheelchair guy, so now we've got a *Rear Window* thing going on, but then the movie cuts to the cat from *Pumpkinhead* and *Millennium,* telling his buddies one of the dumbest, least funny anecdotes I've ever heard, and

I've seen Jay Leno live. (They were free tickets, okay?) Bigfoot kills these idiots, there's more *Rear Window* shit, rock solid babe Tiffany Shepis shows us her tits, Bigfoot kills her, the sheriff refuses a request for help because "that's a good 25-minute ride" (your tax dollars at work), someone mentions the Flatwoods Monster (I'd much rather be watching a movie about the Flatwoods Monster than this), Bigfoot punches a hole in the ceiling and pulls a chick through from the floor above (okay, this part was pretty boss), Bigfoot gets pepper sprayed, a guy's face is bitten off, heaps of abuse is ladled on a blonde mega-hottie (she's a natural, unadjusted 9, for sure, and I *never* award a chick a 9, not even Kimber Riddle, who's a 10), and Bigfoot is finally killed when he's hit by a station wagon, which is almost certainly the way the vast majority of Bigfoots (Bigfeet?) would be killed if they actually existed. The last half hour is serviceable, but aside from Tiffany's tits it's a real slog getting there, and really, you should have better things to do. That tube of cookie dough in the freezer isn't gonna eat itself, you know.

The Abominable Snowman

(1957)

Directed by Val Guest

This one's got a pretty good pedigree, with lots of old-school heavy hitters showing up in the credits, including Grand Moff Tarkin and the guy who wrote the *Quatermass* movies. Grand Moff Tarkin joins up with a stripped-down expedition to find the Yeti, much to his hot-ass wife's chagrin. (Tough break, baby. Just double-down on the life insurance and hope for the best.) The local monks aren't exactly on board either, but they're pacifists so what are they going to do? Hold a sit-in? Write a strongly worded letter to the *Tibetan Times*? Start an online petition? Good luck with that, pacifists. We'll try not to bring too much of the mountain down while we're lobbing grenades at your snow monster. These things never go as planned though, and worse yet these Yetis have some sort of... mystical allure, I guess?... that compels folks to wander off in response to their call and then fall off the mountain to their death. One can only assume that this ability also plays a major role in the Yeti dating scene. The Yeti is pretty underwhelming when they finally deign to show us the damn thing (seriously, they treat it like it's a goddamned state secret or something), and there's a lot of talk, but at least it's interesting talk (as opposed to, say, bickering). Frankly it's all a bit too classy and low-key for my tastes, but this movie is British so I suppose that's to be expected. At least it's not some lost & found footage piece of crap, full of cartoon effects and pissing me off. See below for the cheesy, B-movie knockoff version of this (*The Snow Creature*), which, inexplicably, came out three years previously.

Abominable Snowman

(2013)

Directed by Mark Makilaakso

Yes, shitting on Syphilis (Syfy) Channel Original Movies is like kicking fish in a barrel, but so what? Basic cable isn't fucking free - they owe us a minimal level of entertainment, and when they fail at this monumentally simple task we have every right to call them out, post nasty comments on message boards, and follow the writers and directors around in real life, yelling racial slurs at them while they're trying to pick their kids up from school. In fact, as movie fans, it's not just our right, it's out *duty*. That said, I'm really not in the mood for this movie's generic, lackluster bullshit, so I'll just hit the highlights. The main chick's jeans are ridiculously tight. If you paused the Blu-ray you could probably count her pubes. The cartoon Yeti (because of course it's a cartoon, and it looks like total shit) kills a random and a showboating "rescue team" before our main group of assholes shows up. Their reluctant helicopter pilot only responds to juvenile taunts. There's an avalanche, which the group leader repeatedly refers to as an *avalaunch*. This same tool says that an injured guy is "coughing up a little blood" but is "okay for the most part". Aside from, you know, all that internal bleeding and/or his sudden-onset tuberculous. The Yeti action is a joke. There's no real gore, or tits, or even bad language. For real, this pussified movie would balk at taking extra ketchup packets from the Burger King. By no means is this the worst movie in this book, but it is pretty lame, and since we're still in the A's here I figured I'd better make an example of it. Think of it as the movie critic's equivalent of randomly firing someone your first day on the job.

Ancient Mysteries "Bigfoot"

(1994)

Produced by James P. Taylor Sr.

Does Bigfoot really exist? Short answer: you're a moron. Long answer:

"Either the most complex and sophisticated hoax in the history of anthropology has continued for centuries without being exposed, or the most man-like and largest non-human primate on earth has managed to survive in parts of North America and remains undiscovered by modern science." –G. W. Gill, President of the American Board of Forensic Anthropology

"Sophisticated hoax"??? It's some guy running around it a monkey suit! It never fooled Scooby-Doo and it sure as hell shouldn't fool you, mister so-called anthropologist. Naturally this show is full of cretins who say that Bigfoot can't be a dude in a suit because he would have to be part of some vast "fake Bigfoot" secret society (don't try to follow the logic here; your brain will explode), and pictures of Bigfoot so convincing that they have to draw an outline around where he's supposedly standing before you can even identify the "hulking shape" they're talking about. Oh, and one cat they interview is *literally* identified on screen as a "Story Teller". Uh huh. My favorite though is the complete fag who says that when he "seen" Bigfoot he got so emotional that he started to cry. "To the disbelievers: there's gonna be a, rather a large, hairy surprise one day when somebody finds one," he ~~says~~ lisps. I'll bet you can't wait, queer.

Assault of the Sasquatch

(2009)

Directed by Andrew Gernhard

So, they finally did it. They finally remade *Assault on Precinct 13* with a Sasquatch. At least the Sasquatch isn't a goddamned cartoon, and this movie does have a few cool parts, like when Sassy squashes this yippy little dog, or where he blasts one guy with an entire mailbox. There's lots of gore and crazy violence actually, and even some tits. (The tits only clock in at about average, but I'll take it.) Given this level of insanity I can forgive some unbelievably bad acting (eyepatch guy) and the part where you can see the moviemakers in a window (look behind the cop who gets stabbed in the throat), but what I can't forgive are *the two comedic relief nerds who are trying to get video of the Sasquatch.* For real, these two wretched fucks are annoying beyond belief and they literally cost the movie two stars, one for each of them. Which ultimately puts it at, well, zero stars. Tough break, makers of *Assault of the Sasquatch*. You should've reined those assholes in a little bit. Especially the fat one.

Bigfoot

(1970)

Directed by Robert F. Slatzer

The emblem for the company that made this movie (Gemini-American) (me neither) features two stylized guys who appear to be joined at the dick. We start by meeting the many disparate idiots (bikers, yokels, bleached blondes... every 1970s standard, really) who are destined to be cornholed by Bigfoot. (I mean that symbolically, but the tagline of this movie is "...breeds with anything!" so maybe literally too.) The whole movie has a distinctly *Dukes of Hazzard* vibe to it, comedic and rednecky, but the more-or-less main guy (the shyster salesman) is played by that cat who's in like every old movie ever made and he's a seasoned pro so he buoys the entire production so that it's never *too* painful to watch. Also like *The Dukes of Hazzard*, the villains are presented as a non-jokey, creditable threat but never actually hurt anybody. (The Bigfoots just tie everyone they carry off to a stake, like Indians in an old TV western.) There's a Bigfoot burial ground; the biggest, meanest Bigfoot fights a bear; and there's a scene where two captive chicks calmly discuss their inevitable rape. I was more impressed with the little things though, like the dude who declares that he's not getting involved in any Bigfoot hunt, leaves, and we never see him again. There's always one pussy in every group, and I like that the movie acknowledges this without feeling the need to kill him off later as a punishment.

I also like that the main guy has to tie the door of his station wagon shut with a rope. It all ends with a chase involving Bigfoot, bikers, a one-armed Indian (casino, not 7-11), comedic Southern shysters, and a retarded guy (who, for some reason, is allowed to carry the dynamite), something that could only happen in a movie from 1970. It's not a great Bigfoot movie – in fact, it's pretty stupid – but at least some care went into it; they didn't just run around the woods, screaming and shaking a consumer-grade camera around. Is there such a thing as an F+? If there is, I give it that.

Bigfoot

(2012)

Directed by Bruce Davison

This movie features quite possibly the greatest cast ever assembled, especially if your world stopped in the 1970s. Baby Boomers, I'm looking at you. It's got Danny Partridge, Greg Brady, Aubrey from *Twin Peaks* (now a bull dyke, apparently), Johnny Fever, Alice Cooper, and, of course, Bigfoot. Too bad it's an irredeemably dumb piece of fucking shit. Bigfoot, who's King Kong sized, just rolls in out of nowhere one day, starts trashing everything, punts Alice Cooper several miles (jealous, Marilyn Manson?), and then proceeds to bite multiple folks' heads off, all in response to a 1980s-themed music festival. I guess that makes this ripoff specialists The Asylum's take on *Grizzly 2*, and while it may seem utterly gratuitous and insane to rip off an unreleased sequel so obscure that even a Hollywood insider once told me that it didn't exist, I wouldn't put anything past the company that came up with *Abraham Lincoln vs. Zombies* and *Snakes on a Train*. The obligatory great white hunter is actually black and looks like Barack Obama, the thrill-less climax takes place at Mt. Rushmore (wow, just like *North by Northwest*), Lincoln's head is exploded (emancipate that, asshole), there's a single funny joke ("I came here to promote my book on golf, you know that."), and the production company is called "Smelly Ape, LLC". If any of that makes actually you want to watch this damn thing, it's all on you.

Bigfoot vs D.B. Cooper

(2014)

Directed by David DeCoteau

If you don't know who D. B. Cooper is, correct this immediately, because he was an awesome fucking cat who pulled off one of the greatest capers in American history. Okay, so all evidence suggests that he died as a result, but so what? History doesn't linger on the details. And the idea that he might have met Bigfoot in the process isn't even entirely implausible, if you discount the fact that Bigfoot doesn't actually exist, of course. So it's not a bad ~~premise~~ gimmick, but the joke's on us because the asshat behind this movie is our old friend David DeCoteau, and he's hasn't met a concept yet that can't be boiled down to "...but first there's an hour of gay cheesecake." That's right, the versus doesn't even begin until over an hour into this movie. Until then, it's just scene after scene after scene of a disgusting, sub-human pervert spying on young, shirtless men. (In case it's not clear, I'm referring to David DeCoteau here, not Bigfoot.) And let me tell you, these fine young Turks take shirtless to a whole new level. They hike cross-country shirtless. They answer the door, as a group, shirtless. They go hunting shirtless. They engage in conspiracy to commit air piracy shirtless. They give the director endless behind-the-scenes shoulder massages shirtless. (Probably.) I doubt any of them could even tell you where one *buys* a shirt. (Yes, a couple of shirts do appear in this film, but I'm sure they were gifts.) And even if you're, say, a big NFL fan and enjoy this sort of homoneurotic content, the rest of the movie is still inexcusably cheap and lazy. D. B. Cooper's bomb, for example, appears to be several cardboard paper towel tubes with some twine wrapped around them. Are you fucking kidding me? Even if you do limit yourself to stuff you fished out of the recycle bin, you can easily make a *much* more realistic-looking bomb than that with almost no additional effort, and I should know because that's how I cleared out the Walmart so I could boost the very HDTV I'm currently watching this crummy movie on. Shit like this just goes to show how little respect David DeCoteau has for us, his fucking audience, never mind that without us he'd just be another dirty old man who likes taking pictures of barely-legal boys. Fuck you, DeCoteau, you no-talent shit. If God actually existed, your filmography would be a total affront to him.

Bigfoot Wars

(2014)

Directed by Brian T. Jaynes

This might be an odd thing to say, but I expect a lot from a movie called "Bigfoot Wars". And let's face it, the image that title conjures up is a lot to live up to: an entire herd of Bigfoots rampaging through some isolated mountain town, smashing the shit out of absolutely everything whilst killing and raping with impunity. Hell, throw in a poorly-timed beauty pageant and it could be the Bigfoot version of *Humanoids from the Deep*. That, my friends, that is the fantasy. So what does *Bigfoot Wars* actually deliver? Well a naked hottie in the very first scene is a good start – even if the scene itself is incredibly stupid – and she barely manages to slip into her (sexy) underwear before being dragged off by a Bigfoot. Next on the Bigfoots' hit list: three bikini-clad megahotties and their who cares? boyfriends, with one of these chicks being graphically torn limb-from-limb. So far, so good. From a technical standpoint this movie is a little rough around the edges (that's a nice way of saying it's badly made), but as far as I'm concerned there's enough gore and action to justify its existence. And I must say, I can't remember the last time I saw so many stunningly beautiful actresses in one movie, and they all do a terrific job, too. Contrast this with a supposed "pro" like the kid from *The Hitcher* (1986), who isn't shy about letting us know that he thinks he's too good for this nonsense, despite being best known as the kid from *The Hitcher*. Hell, I can almost hear him now: "Fuck this shit! I was in *The Outsiders*!" Ha ha! Tough break, kid from *The Hitcher*. You can suck it.

Boggy Creek

(2010)

Directed by Brian T. Jaynes

Hmm, two in a row for this Brian T. Jaynes cat, and they both open the same way, with a barely-clad hottie being dragged to her death. Fortunately, those are three of my favorite things, so let's see how this one pans out.

This blonde cutie fucks off to her parents' cabin to reflect on her pop's death, along with her socially-retarded best friend ("You know, Jen, I kinda envy what you have with your dad. I mean, I know he died and all...") and a bunch of unwelcome tag-alongs, all invited by said best friend, who, apparently, is kind of a selfish cunt. One additional problem: there are heart-eating, rape-happy Bigfoots in the woods, something everyone seems to know but no one has any inclination to do anything about. ("I don't want you in the woods, ever!" screams the main chick's dad in a flashback. Or you could, you know, not take her anywhere near there in the first place. Just a suggestion.) Needless to say, the only thing worse than being grabbed by Bigfoot is knowing that, sooner or later, he's going to have sex with you, and with that in mind the last scene in this movie is legitimately horrific and disturbing. Well played. The music throughout is awful though, total *One Tree Hill* type stuff. (Every time a song plays in this movie, I found myself thinking "You've got an important choice to make, Dawson.

One that will impact the rest of your life.") Oh, and one of the actors is named "Texas Battle", and he deserves to be punched in the face just for that, never mind that he's a shitty actor, too. Back to the positives, aside from some crappy editing the movie looks pretty good, slick and professional, which is more than you can say for the original *Boggy Creek* movies. (Seriously, of all the also-ran 1970s horror touchstones to dredge up, *Boggy Creek*? They should've just called this "Bigfoot Rampage" or something.) There's some gore and lots of pretty girls, with the standout, as usual, being the redhead. Too bad she's only in one scene. Oh, and it features a song by Cory Hart! Okay, so it's not the famous Corey Hart (you know; he played for the Brewers), but wouldn't it be hilarious if it was? *"You can never suren-en-der! When you're being gang-raped by Bigfoo-oots!"* Oops, dammit, spoiler warning.

Boggy Creek II: And the Legend Continues...

(1985)

Directed by Charles B. Pierce

So, a gun-toting professor and his three assistants, one of whom is perpetually shirtless (too bad it's the guy) go looking for the Boggy Creek monster, only to be laughed at by the locals, attacked by a rabid dog, and, while they don't actually show this happening, I'm going to assume that one of them got a pretty nasty sunburn. Seriously, put on a shirt, you skinny fucking dork. Eventually they do encounter the monster, but nothing really happens and, ultimately, the whole thing is a complete waste of time. For the uninitiated (you lucky fucks), the Boggy Creek monster was basically a more obscure, redneckier version of Bigfoot, and they made a several movies about him starting in the 1970s because, well, the 1970s. *Boggy Creek II* was the third one (I know, don't ask), and is only notable for a handful of scenes where the submerged monster swims after its unsuspecting victims and pulls them underwater. In fact, these are the only effective scenes in the entire movie, so much so that one might be forgiven for seeing one of them on TV once, out of context, and then spending *twenty years* trying to figure out what movie it was from only to be disappointed to learn that it wasn't some cool, obscure killer fish movie, it was goddamned *Boggy Creek II*. Yeah, yeah, hilarious. Fuck you.

BvZ: Bigfoot vs Zombies

(2016)

Directed by Mark Polonia

As I learn more and more about Bigfoot it becomes apparent that he's really only interested in two things - eluding reality shows, and raping our white women. Maybe that's why Bigfoot movies are so boring; you can only do so much raping and eluding before you're just any given college football player. Fortunately this movie has the good sense to include some chintzy zombies too, and, as promised, it's only a matter of time until they versus. *To the death.* This flick definitely falls on the high end of backyard cinema, but it looks pretty good for all that, even if it is kinda stupid at times. (Seriously, neither of those guys noticed Bigfoot slipping into the back of that jeep? In broad daylight? Two feet away? Fuck the fuck off.) It's the kind of stupid where people tried their best and failed though, not the kind of stupid David DeCoteau cynically grinds out whenever he needs some quick cash to pay off his latest pool boy so he doesn't press charges. There's some pathetically fake gore, the setting (a *CSI*-style body farm) is unique and inexplicably effective, and I like that the mad scientist who created the zombies looks like Dick Van Patten. Ultimately, I have to give it an F, but the kind of F where I get really drunk and take it home anyway, fuck it senseless, and possibly suck on its toes. You know what I'm talking about, right, Michelle?

The Capture of Bigfoot

(1979)

Directed by Bill Rebane

As our movie opens, it seems Bigfoot has already been captured, and I must say, I was quite pleased with the efficiency of their storytelling. It wasn't to last though, because the Bigfoot is quickly rescued by one of his compatriots and... Okay, hold the mayo. These monsters are fucking *white*. I'm sorry, but everyone knows that brown = Bigfoot and white = *Yeti*. Am I wrong here? Tell me if I'm wrong. You can't call your movie *The Capture of Bigfoot* when what they've captured is, in fact, a Yeti, because they're *not the same thing*. It's like saying Mr. Spock and Yoda are completely interchangeable because they're both smart and have pointy ears. What a pair of cosmopolitan Yetis are doing slumming it in the rural backwoods of Hicksconsin is a mystery, but maybe that explains why the (human) bad guy is so keen to capture one of them.

Anyway, the *Yeti* continues to rampage through the forest, attacking random people, but then this movie suddenly decides to take a detour into family-friendly territory, a territory where things generally suck. See there's these two annoying kids, and in an indefensibly deplorable scene one of them crosses paths with a baby Yeti and it smiles at him. And yet me tell you, this baby Yeti's smile is so ham-fistedly cloying that it's like seeing a million Robin Williams movie posters all at once.

The urge to kill the little bastard immediately is so powerful that you might suddenly find yourself standing there holding a half-loaded hunting rifle with no memory of even getting off the couch to go fetch it. Seriously, we are talking *Mac and Me* levels of vileness here, and for once the movie in question agrees with me, because not long after two of the bad guy's minions-for-hire *ruthlessly drop the baby Yeti with a shotgun blast to the chest.* Oh my god, this part is *so fucking awesome.* I watched it like eight times, seriously. Ha ha! Fuck you, Baby Yeti. Naturally the adult Yeti is somewhat less amused, and it should come as no surprise that the Yeti attacks continue, leading to this absurd exchange:

SHERIFF: "This thing's got to be killed."

YETI APOLOGIST DOUCHEBAG (PROBABLY VOTED FOR OBAMA): "Why? Because it scares people?"

No, you human dick, because it's *mauling the shit out of people.* Seriously, what a cocksucker. Eventually the human bad guy captures the adult Yeti, but then these other fuck-knockers decide to set it free. (I forget, exactly, what their connection to the Yeti was, or why they were so keen to Free Willy the bastard - this movie is full of so many unnecessary, peripheral characters that I lost track of at least twenty of them). Then, as you'd expect, it all ends with a car chase, explosions, and a fist fight. But wait, there's more! The sheriff is a complete moron who does terrible Bogart impressions (he's an annoying asshole); the main bad guy punches one of his men so hard that the guy flies right through a window and lands outside; at one point the main bad guy literally cackles like a supervillain after coming up with a particularly nefarious plan; there's a disco party (Hear one new disco tune!) (oh, and random hottie shout-out to the disco party girl with the long black hair and white sweater who appears to have a chipped tooth: you're one foxy mama, baby); several people are tied to trees; George "Buck" Flower is bounced off the hood of a car; and in one scene, for absolutely no reason, there's an asshole dressed as a clown on the slopes, dancing around like a fucktard.

So yeah, it's pretty entertaining.

Creature from Black lake

(1976)

Directed by Joy Houck, Jr.

Two jokers go looking for the legendary Creature of Black Lake, AKA Bigfoot. Lots of wandering around and public mockery ensues, there's a sexy waitress, and they're warned off the case by the local sheriff, who's such a goddamned hayseed that he makes Sheriff Lobo look like a big-city so-fist-de-cate by comparison. The rest of the locals are equally evasive. As one puts it: "We don't want nobody snoopin' around heeya makin' us look like a bunch of dumb rednecks!" In fact, they get almost no cooperation at all until they decide to offer a cash re-ward for information: twenty-five American dollars! This is what finally convinces one geezer (played by the cat who played Ornery Camp Cook in every cowboy movie ever made) to tell what he knows, but first he breaks out his harmonica and plays our main guys a little country music! Seriously, how do they even expect to *recognize* the monster amongst all these knuckle-draggers? The geezer's flashbacks are pretty hilarious (Bigfoot hurling a dog halfway across the front yard is a highlight), but all his encounters with the monster took place years ago so his addle-brained remembrances really aren't much help.

The two main guys decide to kill some time trying to score with a couple of Hee Haw Honeys, only to get cockblocked first by the Creature, and then by the sheriff, who, seein' as one of the honeys in question is his daughter, arrests the both of them. God and bad screenwriters move in mysterious ways though, because while in jail they finally meet someone who's seen Bigfoot recently, played by that cat who played Grizzled Prospector in pretty much every applicable movie ever made, and he finally puts them on the monster's trail. At one point one of the main dudes is startled when something big, hairy, and bipedal sneaks up on him while he's pissing in the woods. Holy shit, is it the Creature? Nope - it's a beaded, stoned-out hippie! That's the kind of idiot fake-out this movie banks on (later, this same guy is terrified by a mule), that is when it's not going on unrelated tangents like the part where a fart joke sets one of the guys off about 'Nam. (Dear everyone who was in 'Nam: No one cares. Shut the fuck up about it already.) Nevertheless, when Bigfoot finally does show himself he goes absolutely bug-shit crazy, spaz-attacking these two fools like a boogie woogie Bigfoot boy from company B, rolling entire vans down hills, the works. It's *almost* worth the time it takes to get there.

In the ~~anals~~ annals of terrible 1970s Bigfoot movies (and they're all terrible), *Creature from Black Lake* is one of the few that in any way delivers, despite the rip-off title, the inevitable redneck vibe (if you watched a lot of trucker shows in the 1970s, you'll recognize several more faces here), and the fact that there's an actor named "Roger Pancake" in it. While you could clearly do a lot better, you could probably do a lot worse, too.

Cry Wilderness

(1987)

Directed (in the loosest sense of the term) by Jay Schlossberg-Cohen

This detestable little cockrag is spinning implausible yarns about chugging Coca-Cola and listening to rock music with Bigfoot, and he even believes that Bigfoot visits him at night, calling out his name beneath his bedroom window like a jilted bro who's downed too many Jägerbombs. Warned by "Bigfoot" that his dad is in trouble, he runs away from school and hitches his way home. (Catching rides with strangers is fun kids, try it!) Once there he's almost shot when he surprises his forest ranger dad in the woods, then he torments the wildlife for a while (chasing a wild bobcat, sneaking up on a skunk in the woods) (harassing skunks is fun kids, try it!) before they head home, where two "pet" raccoons are allowed to run wild, utterly trashing the place while a (possibly retarded) Indian (casino, not 7-11) watches, laughing like a goon. Oh, and occasionally a musclebound rageaholic will invite himself in, help himself to some grub, and try to strangle one of the raccoons to death with his bare hands, just for the hell of it. It's the kind of home life that's begging for the Department of Social Services to get involved, but there's no time for that because suddenly this movie decides that it wants to be a ripoff of *Jaws* (or at least *Grizzly*). See, the Twelve Pines Summer Resort is about to open for the season, and the owner can't have

Bigfoot wandering around, being all elusive and undetectable and shit. So he orders the forest ranger, the retarded Indian, and a big-game hunter to track Bigfoot down down and kill it. They quickly locate Bigfoot's cave (which is surrounded by so much litter that I'm surprised the Indian didn't start to cry), but Bigfoot evades them, fleeing into the... er, day. Now it's fucking on, or it would be if this movie wasn't such a tepid, scatterbrained piece of crap. There's a time-killing detour to an animal rehabilitation clinic; a Bengal tiger suddenly crashes the party for no logical reason ("That must be the tiger that escaped from the circus!" exclaims one guy, after the fact. I guess that clears *that* up.); a ghost appears to offer some advice; the Indian confirms that he's retarded when he says "It's rock and roll music!" (you'll have to hear this part to understand; it's all in the delivery); and in the end the human bad guy is gruesomely blinded, a scene that I appreciated but which is hilariously out-of-place in such a kiddie-oriented flick. The story is dumber than a bag of sand, the acting is some of the worst on record (the three drunk bikers who appear in one scene seem to have "acting" confused with "palsy"), it's boring, and how many "kids befriend Bigfoot" movies does the world need, anyway? If you ask me, one is too many. Especially if it's this one.

Curse of Bigfoot

(1975)

Directed by Don Fields

Okay, why would you open a movie with a bunch of obvious day-for-night shots – complete with some typical frog/night bird nighttime sound effects – and include shots of the *sun?* At any rate, a monster is lurking out there in the night(?), and it quickly (in a relative sense, of course) claims its first victim, an androgynous nitwit who I'm pretty sure was just about to start humping his/her dog. Then the lights come up, because it turns out that this was just a movie the worst high school teacher in the world was showing to his class! "You stopped it at the best part!" one student complains. Uh oh. But class isn't over yet. Next up is a guest speaker, who, after a lengthy introduction involving tons of stock footage, flashbacks, a detour for an unrelated Q&A session, and plenty of incoherent rambling, finally tells us all about the time he encountered Bigfoot. Seems one day he was out in the hills, prying up ancient caveman tablets with some of his archaeology students, when underneath one of these they discovered Bigfoot! Except it's *not* Bigfoot, it's a mummy. I mean, one guy (who was introduced to us as an expert of some sort, on something or other) even says, and I quote, "It's a mummy." That night the mummy pops back to life and kills somebody, so our main peeps decide to set a trap for it. Since this trap involves proven idiots and several cans of gasoline I was eagerly waiting for it to backfire hilariously, but it doesn't and this flick ends just as lamely as it began. Let's face it, the real curse of Bigfoot is that 99% of his movies suck, and this one is no exception, but aside from documentaries at least he has the decency to show up in his other films. Of course with all the tangentially-related flashbacks and dicking around at least half of this movie doesn't have any bearing on itself anyway, so I guess I shouldn't be too surprised that even the titular (heh) character got lost along the way.

Demonwarp

(1988)

Directed by Emmett Alston

I write books about a wide range of subjects, as long as that subject is movies: ghost movies, zombie movies, UFO movies... The best thing about *Demonwarp* is that I could have included it in any or all of my books and it wouldn't be out of place. And, as you can imagine, the *worst* thing about *Demonwarp* is second verse, same as the first. It's got a hysterical Bigfoot home invasion (two, actually; the second time, I think Bigfoot steals their toaster); gore; one nice set of tits (yes, I know three different girls go topless in this movie; you figure it out); and a kid who looks and acts like an even douchier Kirk Cameron, which is no mean feat seeing as Kirk Cameron has long been recognized as the peak of human douchitude to the point where everything he touches literally turns into a giant douche. And yes I'm using the word *literally* properly in this context. For the first hour or so it's basically just a Bigfoot movie, although Bigfoot seems particularly pissed off this time around, snapping necks, tearing heads off, and using a stick to stir a guy's guts while they're still inside the guy's body. But then Bigfoot's victims start coming back as zombies, and when our default main guy follows one of these zombies into a mysterious cave (hey, zombified or not she's still the hottest piece of ass around) he finds an alien spaceship full of aliens (okay, fine, there's one alien) because, apparently, it's all the work of aliens. (You win this round, Giorgio A. Tsoukalos.) (You're still a racist sack of shit, though.) The theories of John Keel notwithstanding, there's just no way to reconcile all this insanity into a single, coherent whole, and despite it all *Demonwarp* still manages to be kind of boring. Clearly the people who dreamed up this flick just hijacked the premise of the Bigfoot episode of The Six Million Dollar Man and took it to its... well, *logical* definitely isn't the right word here, so let's say *inevitable* conclusion. Which is why it's a blessing that that show never had a sixth season.

Devil on the Mountain

(2006)

Directed by Steven R. Monroe

You know where else the devil is? In the details. And the details are that this movie has shitty editing (especially during the action scenes; good luck figuring out what, exactly, is supposed to be going on), no gore, no tits, too much fucking talk, and a weird dead zone in the middle where the action just stops while everyone holes up for the night to engage in a bunch of unrealistic bonding and soul-searching, then picks right up again in the morning, as if everyone, including Bigfoot, mutually agreed to take an extended coffee break. It's a shame, because the first half of this movie isn't too bad, and it's got the main cat from *Pumpkinhead* and *Millennium* (he even makes a *Pumpkinhead* reference at one point) **and** Jack Deth in it. (Jack gets the best line when he mentions that his hunting dogs are at the vet: "I'm sure they're flyin' high on some kinda dog dope...") Some of the other characters are passably amusing too, like the bank robber who keeps making stock trades right in the middle of a shootout, or the one who's late for the robbery because he's busy banging an ugly waitress in the restaurant stockroom. Seriously, dude, if you can't manage your time better than this, set an alarm on your phone or something. And while we're on the subject of people who are inexcusably bad at their jobs, could someone out there – a trusted family member, maybe – please tell "cinematographer" Neil Lisk to *stop shaking the* *goddamned camera around?* Stupid asshole. Final answer, this movie kinda blows. But it didn't *entirely* piss me off, and when you're dealing with me sometimes that's the best you can hope for.

Drawing Flies

(1996)

Directed by Malcolm Ingram and Matt Gissing

Once again, here's a movie that epically fails the Mr. Satanism Movie Title Acid Test. Far more off-putting than the title though is the introduction by the director (well, one of them, anyway) and Silent Bob that opens the DVD. It's an endless, rambling nightmare that feels way, way longer than it probably is WHY WON'T THEY SHUT UP AND GET ON WITH IT STFU SILENT BOB. Finally, weeks later, the actual movie begins and while I was prepared to hate the fuck out of it I have to admit it isn't half bad. Or all bad, even. In fact, it's actually pretty good. A bunch of broke, pop culture-dissecting, Gen X fucks are about to be evicted, so they piss off to this cabin in the woods where they figure they can squat until they get their shit together, which, being Gen Xers, will probably happen right about the time Obama is sworn into office. Turns out there is no cabin though - their by-default leader made the whole thing up and engineered this trip solely so he could look for Bigfoot. Imagine if the guys from *Clerks* (1994) walked off the job to look for Bigfoot, and that's basically this movie. I know that sounds terrible, but trust me, I've seen scores of movies about assholes traipsing through the woods looking for Bigfoot (come to think of it, most of those were probably documentaries, but whatever), and believe it or not this really is one of the better ones. If nothing else there's a Pearl Jam diss early on (almost no one – besides me – had the balls to call out critical and proto-hipster darlings Pearl Jam in 1996, so kudos to this movie for suggesting that they suck), and the chicks are fucking HOT, which should come as no surprise since this movie is Canadian and Canadian chicks are the Western hemisphere's unsung goddesses. Canadian chicks, I love you. *Drawing Flies*, I liked you. Pearl Jam, you can deep-throat a diseased one. Like with sores all over it and shit.

Frostbite!

(2012)

Directed by David Hicks

This starts with an old lady kicking Bigfoot in the nuts and a fat guy farting in someone's face. Fans of *Impractical Jokers* will be ecstatic. They'll probably start jerking off. Those of us with a measurable I.Q., on the other hand, will hate every second of this unfunny piece of shit. In fact, the only reason I kept watching it instead of making up a totally imaginary 1970s Bigfoot movie to fill this slot (I was torn between *Disco Sasquatch* and *Bruce Lee Against Bigfoot*) is because it features *Ginger Snaps'* Katharine Isabelle, one of Canada's greatest non-Shatner thespian exports and one of the tastiest chicks in all recorded history. The plot, #6A, is the old "friends throw a party to save a failing business from an evil developer" shtick, which is a perfectly fine cliche to hang a movie on because everybody likes parties and nobody has liked evil developers since at least *Poltergeist* (1982). The problem is that this stupid, terrible movie isn't funny AT ALL. And I don't mean it's just a little bit not funny. It's not funny like the phrase "inoperable cancer" isn't funny. It's not funny like backing over a beloved family pet in the driveway isn't funny. It's not funny like outliving your children isn't funny. I'm not exaggerating when I say that this is, bar none, the worst Canadian movie I have ever seen, and, not counting found footage movies (which don't count anyway), one of the ten worst I've ever seen, period. And

I attend film festivals. It's just an endless parade of people being hit in the balls, and their sorry-ass idea of a big guest star is fucking *Snow*, AKA the even less talented Canadian equivalent of Vanilla Ice that 90% of you probably had to look up just now to even know who I'm talking about. Seriously, there is no reason to make jokes about Snow outside of the ten week window when he was actually on the pop culture radar, and even then it was kind of pointless because he was such an easy target. Bigfoot's contribution, meanwhile, is limited to stealing beer (off camera) and fucking a fat guy up the ass. Katharine, you're awesome, but you owe me dinner, at least, for sitting through this one. You deserve better. Canada deserves better. We all deserve better.

The Geek

(1971)

Produced by Brutus Productions

"His feet aren't the only thing that's big." That's not this movie's tagline, but it should have been. Three dorks are out to photograph Bigfoot, accompanied by three chicks who the narrator assures us are only there to be passed around like a syphilitic joint. Looks like Gloria Steinem happened just in time. The first chick is actually pretty cute and has great tits. She fucks her husband early on and later is raped by Bigfoot. Chick number two, the blonde, is no great shakes; the best I can say about her is that she'd do in a pinch. She also fucks her man at one point, but avoids being raped by Bigfoot. Our final chick is the least attractive, and she doesn't even get to fuck her date before being raped by Bigfoot. Of course, given her date's awful Monkees haircut and dorky medallion, whether she's actually worse off for this is up for debate. Fortunately, both of our victimized chicks are pretty stoic about being ravaged by Bigfoot. Frankly, the cute one looks kinda bored. When it's all over, one of the dudes vows to "get that filthy animal" someday, but since he didn't do squat to help the girls at the time I can only assume that his belated plan is to locate and fuck *Bigfoot's* girlfriend in a sort of inter-species tit-for-tat. Kind of makes you glad they never shot a sequel, although come to think of it we don't know that for sure and we'll probably never know, since there's no end credits to help us identify the people responsible, which doubly sucks because I'd love to track these actresses down and show this movie to their grandkids. I can hear their lame-ass excuses already. "I was young and I needed… actually they paid me in dope, so never mind."

Note: At least one (human-on-human) blowjob seems to have been cut out of this movie. In the interests of good taste, I guess.

Harry and the Hendersons

(1987)

Directed by William Dear

The problem with all these Bigfoot horror movies is that Bigfoot just isn't scary. Think about it. If you looked out your window and saw Bigfoot rolling down the street *right now* you might be a little surprised, but would you piss yourself in terror? Of course not, because Bigfoot looks like a monkey, and all our lives we've been taught that monkeys are lovable clowns who exist to entertain us. It's really not that hard to imagine someone training Bigfoot to smoke cigars or ride a little bicycle or dump a beer all over Deputy Perkins. The people who made this flick were smart enough to know that much at least, so they dusted of the old E.T./Johnny 5/ALF template, used the 1987 version of find/replace (commonly known as "an intern") to substitute "Bigfoot", and came up with a "cute" Bigfoot movie that sucks in entirely different and original ways. Seriously, a family hits Bigfoot with their car and then *takes it home with them?* I mean, if they were gonna freeze it because they didn't want to waste the meat that would be one thing, but this Bigfoot is still alive and the big gag is that it crashes at their pad for a while and becomes their friend. It's so fucking stupid that it buggers the imagination. And how fucking obvious and lazy is it that they have to hide Bigfoot from an annoying neighbor who keeps showing up? Or that there's a bad guy on their trail who wants to shoot Bigfoot? In fact, the worst thing about this movie is how many times Bigfoot has a gun pointed at him but never actually gets popped. Christ, I wanted someone to blow that miserable bastard's head off **so fucking bad.** Every time it *nearly* happened was like a chick sucking you *allllllmost* to climax and then punching you in the balls instead. And don't even get me started on the *really* stupid shit, like the part where Bigfoot howls like a police siren so the good guys can get through traffic. Christ, Hollywood, why don't you just drop by my house and tell me that you think I'm an asshole to my face? Fuck you.

I did like the teenage daughter though. I've definitely got something big and legendary for her, if she wants to see it.

Howls

(2011)

Directed by Jamie Tracey

I'm beginning to accept the fact that there's never been a truly great Bigfoot movie, and I doubt there ever will be. The Yeti, maybe, because he lives over in Europe or China or someplace and as a result he at least seems kind of exotic. But Bigfoot? Bigfoot is just too steeped in 1970s' redneck culture, like CB radios or a Barbara Mandrell and the Mandrell Sisters Christmas Special. That said, this Bigfoot movie, created by a guy with two girls' names and, as far as I can tell, released directly to YouTube, might just be the worst one ever made, in large part because the plot, like Bigfoot, doesn't even exist. Three unlikable assholes – Dane Cook Wannabe, Ponytail McDouchebag, and Relatively Normal Guy But Fuck Him Anyway – who are apparently friends but clearly hate each other, go looking for a missing dog. They wander around yelling the dog's name for what feels like hours but in reality was probably only fifteen solid minutes of screen time. (Incidentally, IIRC, the dog's name was 'Fuck This Movie'.) Eventually Dane Cook Wannabe and Ponytail O'Douchebag get lost in the woods, because they're stupid, and oh my god I'm having *Blair Witch* flashbacks, although at least *Blair Witch* had a cute chick in it. So they walk and walk and walk and walk and Jesus Christ how far are we into this awful movie. Forty-five minutes??? Fuck almighty, kill me now. For real, this might just be the most nothing I have ever seen in a movie, and I'm including the one Andy Warhol made that's just five hours of some guy sleeping when I say that. In fact, sometimes this movie is kinda like one of those novelty Warhol films, like the part where they hold this shot of a house for a full twenty seconds while absolutely nothing happens.

Okay, so we're an hour in now and absolutely nothing has happened except for three guys strolling around and repeatedly yelling "Cuntfuck!" (I've decided that should be the dog's name.) Believe it or not Bigfoot does eventually make an appearance, but it should come as no surprise to anyone that when he finally shows up he just walks around and around, doing nothing. Monkey see, monkey do, I guess. In the end, he just looks at the main guys for a few seconds and then walks away, just like you should look at the poster for this movie or the DVD and just walk away. Fuck you, Jamie Tracey, you cocksucker whorefuck. Fuck you for wasting my time, and nine other people's (maybe), with your bullshit hoax of a non-movie. You know what your next project should be, you miserable, no-talent ass sandwich? A documentary about everyone who sat through *this* movie lining up and punching you in the face. Rest assured, I'd watch that one until the goddamned DVD wore out. Fuck you.

The Legend of Bigfoot

(1975)

Directed by Harry Stuart Winer

Again with the trying to prove the existence of Bigfoot. Or, as my people call him, maize. Honestly, if you really believe that there's a huge ape-like monkey living in the woods of America despite the fact that no one's ever taken a picture of one, found a dead one, discovered any bones of one, been friended on Facebook by one, or even turned up the inevitable sick fuck who claims to have had sex with one, you truly are a grade-A moron. The dude behind this docu-flick wouldn't take moron for an answer though, so he bought a movie camera and went looking for Bigfoot himself. Now, Bigfoot is notoriously difficult to capture on film because he doesn't exist, but over the years this guy managed to do it like fifty times. I wouldn't be surprised if he had footage of Bigfoot's last family reunion, or pictures of him at the senior prom. The fact that it all looks totally fake? Well, the guy who made this movie is no longer with us, but if he were I'm sure he'd explain that by telling you to go fuck yourself. It's padded with some pretty good wildlife footage though, the most memorable being this bit where a little squirrel keeps trying to wake up his squirrel friend after it gets run over by a car. If you want to make a girl cry and don't feel like hitting her, I guarantee this scene will do the trick. I doubt it will make her believe in Bigfoot though.

The Legend of Boggy Creek

(1972)

Directed by Charles B. Pierce

Great. A monster movie that claims to be a true story AND is rated G. Even fucking *Harry and the Hendersons* was edgy enough to earn a "Parental Guidance Suggested". This was the first most people had ever heard of the Boggy Creek monster, AKA the Fouke Monster, not to be confused with the fuck monster, which is of course me. In a stab at "authenticity" (translation: they couldn't afford real actors) most of the cast is made up of genuine local yokels, but they're some of the few people who are in no position to think that they're above this material so to their credit they actually do a passable job. The people on the other side of the camera, not so much. Almost every scene looks like shit, amateurish and too dark, with a semi-documentary vibe that doesn't really excuse the incompetence but does give them an opening to incorporate interviews with several drunks/liars who claim to have seen the monster. One supposed witness even gets his own theme song ("Hey, Travis Crabtree") which plays over footage of him wandering around in the woods, doing nothing for several minutes (way to waste our time, movie) and was doubtlessly the highlight of his entire hick life. A more motivated reviewer might Google-stalk this guy and see what he's up to today, but I can already make a pretty educated guess without doing all that work - he's fucking drunk. I did respect one old coot they talked to though, who, after living alone in the bog for twenty years, says he's never seen the monster, because it doesn't exist. Good for you, buddy. As for our movie version of the monster, it kills a kitten (by "scaring it to death"), some hogs, and a dog, and, proving that it has at least some intelligence, terrorizes two hot young MILFs and crashes a teenage girls' slumber party. Only at the very end does it attack a person, and while this scene is undeniably hilarious it's hardly worth the slog it takes to get there. Me, I envy that old coot who's never seen the monster. I wish I'd never seen its terrible movie.

Lost Woods

(2012)

Directed by Phillip Ellering and Nathan Ellering

Five jokers go camping (why one of them is dressed for a retro/ 1980s party is never explained), and then that's exactly what happens: they're camping. And chit-chatting. And target-shooting some beer bottles. (Incidentally, you're supposed to open them and drink the beer first, idiots.) And tiptoeing around an incident involving some fireworks that took place over a decade ago and everyone should just get the fuck over already. Look, producers of *Lost Woods*, no one has ever watched a Bigfoot movie because they cared about the characters and yours isn't going to be the first so could we get on with it, please? *Finally* one of them is impale-murdered, but remember we're supposed to *care* about these drips so now everyone is moping and reminiscing and doing everything *but* hiking to the nearest phone to call the authorities. (I'm just taking it for granted that "There's no cell phone reception out here!") That night though Bigfoot finally stops wasting our time, belatedly strolling (rather arrogantly, I might add) into the movie and doling out some onscreen whup-ass. Glasses Guy is dragged off, probably for butt sex. The sole chick is accidentally shot. (Pity. She wasn't half bad.) Mustache Guy is clotheslined by Bigfoot and then Bigfoot just straight beats the shit out of him. Glasses Guy reappears, but he never says that Bigfoot *didn't* butt rape him so I'm still going to assume that's what happened. Minority Guy has a flashback and does some soul searching, because apparently this movie feels that it hasn't wasted enough of our time already. Glasses Guy starts spitting up blood. (Bigfoot's gigantic member probably ruptured something up there, causing internal bleeding.) Glasses Guy's spine is broken. Minority guy kicks Bigfoot in the balls. Bigfoot goes all Apollo Creed on Minority Guy's ass. Minority Guy decapitates Bigfoot with a machete. Then a completely unrelated character shoots lightning out of his face and flies off into outer space, I think? Seriously, I have no idea what's supposed to be happening at the end of this movie. Good thing I really don't give a shit.

The Mummy: Tomb of the Dragon Emperor

(2008)

Directed by Rob Cohen

You mothercunting fuckbombs. You miserable piss mongers. *The Mummy Returns* was a hopeless ball of fuck, but I was willing to give this one a chance because at least they put a different spin on it. As it turns out though, I should've just dropped a dead skunk into a burlap sack, pissed all over it, and then mailed it to myself because this movie is such a piece of shit it's like someone took a shit and then shoved it back up their ass and shit it out again. No, wait, it's more like when a dog takes a shit, eats it, and then shits the exact same shit a second time. It's shit to the second power.

After some nonsensical *Shogun* style backstory, we join the main guy from the first two movies. He's fishing, see, but he can't catch anything so finally he just blows some fish out of the water with a handgun! Ha ha! It's completely illegal and incredibly dangerous! Later of course his wife – who thinks he caught the fish legitimately – eats one and finds a bullet in her mouth. Oh, the wackiness! Before we laugh ourselves to death over all this hilarity the main guy and his wife are off to China, where, in a zany scene rivaling the best of *Three's Company*, they bump into their grown-up son, who's an archaeologist now! It's like a total homage to *Indiana Jones 4*, which, you may recall, is the most hated installment in that series. Maybe they thought they could make this movie look better by reminding us of one that most people dislike even more, but I wasn't taken in by their ruse and all it did was help focus my anger even more on this piece of crap.

So anyway, there's a mummy, and our crew of assclowns (they've also picked up the main chick's brother and a girl ninja by this point) decides to track it down. Along the way there's a car/chariot chase (I like how the bad guys don't kill anybody during this scene, but the good guys shoot off a rocket that blows up a whole trolley car full of innocent bystanders), more awful jokes (a yak pukes, so the brother says "The yak yacked." Please die, all of you.), and, in quite possibly the stupidest goat-fucking bullshit cunt scene to ever appear in any movie that will ever exist and fuck you, a bunch of *abominable snowmen* show up out of nowhere, for absolutely no reason, to lend a hand. (The main guy seems *really* surprised when this happens, like even more than he obviously should be, which is saying a lot. Listen to the way the actor says *"Abominable snowmen???"* when he first sees them. It's like you can *hear* his spirit break at that exact moment. "My career ends here," he's probably thinking. "Oh God, why did I take this role? Oh holy Jesus fuck...")

Honestly, that's it. I can't go on. Not only does the mastermind behind this movie deserve a week-long ass beating, but his whole family deserves an equal amount of grief for raising him to be the type of oblivious, amoral prick who would actually inflict it on the public. If I had my way I'd kick his dad's ass too, then I'd bitch slap his mom, run over his dog, and take his sister out on a date, act like I'm totally into her, then never call her again so she's all like "I don't understand, what did I do wrong?" Seriously, the last time I was this pissed off at a movie I was in it and the lead detective was saying "Looks like we caught you red-handed, Mr. Satanism." *Fuck*.

Night Claws

(2012)

Directed by David A. Prior

Hey, it's Captain America! The shitty one from the 1970s! And Rocky Balboa's mediocre musician brother! Looks like they brought in all the heavy hitters that scale plus all-day access to the food truck could buy. Ha ha! I kid, I kid. Frank Stallone was in *Hudson Hawk*, which is an underrated classic, and Reb "Craptain Americrap" Brown has been in all sorts of fantastic/hilarious junk, like *Yor: The Hunter from the Future* and *Howling II: Your Sister is a Werewolf Bitch*. Plus the guy who did the music is the cat responsible for *Weird TV*, and therefore one of my personal heroes. Seriously, the potential for awesome is almost through the roof. Of course, this assumes that questionable nostalgia and workmanlike music are the two most important factors here, and since this is a monster movie, not VH1 Classic, that couldn't be more wrong. This movie's full of obnoxious dicks who hate each other on sight (I can certainly sympathize); the lazy-ass story lazily rips off ~~Grizzly (1976)~~ *Jaws* (1975) (sorry about your fucking Pumpkin Festival, dude); the writing and acting are strictly open mic night; the chicks are all way too old; we never see any of their draggy-ass mom tits anyway; there's a character named "Cooter" ("Where might I find someone named 'Cooter'?" an out-of-towner asks. Pick any shitty redneck movie, lady.); and is it just me or is Reb "The Sheriff" Brown stoned in every single scene he appears in? Lucky him. Oh, and I would be totally remiss if I didn't mention the instantly infamous scene where the main chick gives the sheriff her business card and it's unmistakably a Monopoly "Get Out Of Jail, Free" card. Are you seriously telling me that no one on this *professional movie shoot* was carrying an actual business card they could use here? Jesus fucking Christ.

Night of the Demon

(1980)

Directed by James C. Wasson

Before we even see the title, Bigfoot (who has glaucoma) rips a guy's arm off and the oozing stump slowly fills one of his trademark footprints with blood. I am instantly in love with this movie. Later Bigfoot gorily smears a dude all over a van; swings a guy in a sleeping bag around and around over his head and then lets him fly, impaling him on a tree branch (Jason Voorhees clearly borrowed this move for *Part VII*); tears a guy's dick off; kills a fool with his own axe; hilariously slaughters two Girl Scouts (Why are you stabbing yourselves? Why are you stabbing yourselves? Ha ha!); rapes a chick (And knocks her up! Better start looking for a second job, Bigfoot.); chokes a bitch 'til she spits up blood; pulls a guy's intestines out... Holy shit, this is it, *THIS IS REALLY IT:* the old-school Bigfoot gore movie we were all dreaming of while we slogged through *Return to Boggy Creek*, but assumed didn't actually exist. And that's not all: there's also the world's shortest (and most realistic) lost & found footage movie, a gory dream sequence, some tits, hypnosis, a Bigfoot cult, grave robbing, and a gruesome patricide. Some of the acting is pretty bad, but who gives a shit? Anyone who would complain about that under these circumstances shouldn't be watching this movie in the first place, they should be out buying napkin rings with their frigid fiancee or something. This is the only essential movie in this entire book. See it, see it even if you have to quit your job, leave your spouse, and abandon your current life entirely. I'm not sure why you'd have to do all that though. It's probably on YouTube.

Prey for the Beast

(2007)

Directed by Brett Kelly

One of the biggest problems with Bigfoot/Yeti movies is their lack of variety. Our central player looks kind of like a gorilla crossed with a caveman, he lives in the woods, and he's either brown or white. And no one ever strays too far from this tired-ass template. Here's the thing, though: Bigfoot is fucking imaginary (yes, he is) (you're an idiot), so who's to say he *doesn't* look like the giant boar from *Razorback* (1984) ass-raped Chewbacca and, defying all logic, they had a baby? It's Pigfoot! And he's a force to be baconed with. The end result is kind of like watching Bebop from *Teenage Mutant Ninja Turtles* go on a gory killing spree, and don't even pretend you never wanted to see that. There's some pretty good lines too, way more than I would have expected. ("*Predator* without weapons is... *Deliverance*.") ("You don't look so good.") So this movie isn't entirely without hope, but the gore is too fake, the acting is fucking terrible ("Kill me. I can't take it."), and there's no tits, so I guarantee that there are still better ways to spend your time. Perhaps a meal at a middling family restaurant? Or maybe that guitar guy is still playing acoustic Human League covers in front of the gas station. Just a suggestion.

Primal

(2007)

Directed by Steffen Schlachtenhaufen

What is with the blonde at the beginning of this flick? She's hot, but her smallish, perky tits are located dead center in the middle of her torso, and the entire time she was onscreen all I could think was "Please, please take off your shirt. I want a better look at this anatomical oddity." [Addendum: If you're thinking of using that as a pickup line, don't.] Anyway, months after this chick and her friends are killed, raped (I assume), and eaten (probably) by Bigfoot, eight more chuckleheads invade his turf, and he makes short work of most of them, too. He polishes them off so quickly, in fact, that this movie has to repeatedly introduce new characters for him to kill, which is particularly hilarious since it's supposed to be taking place in the middle of nowhere, on government land where no trespassing is permitted. Aside from one cute chick in her underwear, and another chick smacked across the kisser with a big stick (she had it coming), there's not much to see here, although I did laugh when the park ranger casually rolled a 1000+ lb. Sasquatch carcass over with his foot, and when they namechecked a character called "Old Salty" who apparently mistook the middle of the wilderness for the ocean. Ultimately, the cleverest thing about this movie is the end credits, which identify all the actors and crew via "missing" posters. (Wishful thinking?) I also liked their jokey implication that this movie was, in fact, produced by a Labrador Retriever. That would explain a lot.

Rage of the Yeti

(2011)

Directed by David Hewlett

Alright, so these folks are tramping around a remote Arctic island after scooping up this rare historic codex (or the "giant book" as one prole calls it) for their obscenely rich employer when they're suddenly attacked by a whole park of cartoon Yetis, whose unique *Predator* fur (unique if you ignore the fact that the *Predator* movies exist, I mean) makes them all but invisible in the snowy landscape. How. Fucking. Convenient. For the production company's bottom line, at least. When we do see the Yetis they naturally look like fake shit (although the overall design is admittedly kinda cool, sort of a cross between a gorilla and a polar bear), which is a shame because aside from that this is actually a pretty decent movie, especially considering its origins (the Syphilis Channel). It's witty and fun without being jokey, the two main guys are cool and likable, and even the rich boss – who would be portrayed as either a coward or a ruthless dick in most movies – comes across as a pretty awesome guy. With real special effects (and maybe some juicier gore) (and some tits) this could have been a minor classic, but as-is it's still really good. It's a rare triumph for the Syphilis Channel, and I would totally watch a sequel starring these characters. Too bad the entirely of their Syfy Original Movie budget is tied up in *Sharknados 6-10*.

Return to Boggy Creek

(1977)

Directed by Tom Moore

Claiming to have seen Bigfoot is as much a redneck touchstone as pining for that fancy new double-wide or going temporarily blind after slurping bad shine out of your cousin's navel. (In your defense, she is pretty hot.) But if you really wanna out-white trash your neighbors and/or your "kin", consider kicking it ~~up~~ down a notch and claiming you saw the Skunk Ape, or, better yet, the Fouke Monster AKA the Legend of Boggy Creek. There are several Boggy Creek Monster movies, and of all of them this one was the hardest to find a copy of pre-Internet, and as you can imagine that's not because it's really good. It's basically a family-friendly/humorous take on the subject, sort of a proto-*Harry and the Hendersons* except imagine that Harry has a (mostly unwarranted) reputation for killing people. It's an absolutely awful movie, padded beginning to end with annoying hick antics perpetrated by people with names like "Crawdad Charlie" and "Billy-John Thumbfuck". One knuckle-dragging asswipe even squanders some of the running time by telling these hicklings the Cajun version of "Hansel and Gretel", which is similar to the original except that the characters are all swamp trash. The sole point of interest is that the main kid is played by a prepubescent Kimberly Drummond, whose tits and ass would go on to be the best things about the sitcom *Diff'rent Strokes* and a few terrible movies before tragically dying before I could make sweet, sweet love to her. Rest in peace, Kimberly. Our loss is Sitcom Heaven's gain.

Sasquatch Hunters

(2005)

Directed by Fred Tepper

This movie does have two things immediately going for it. One is that it is, indeed, a movie, and not a reality show where gullible white trash morons really look for Bigfoot. Two is that it's not a lost & found footage deal. Beyond that though it's as generic as they come. It probably took an afternoon to write. The monsters are tossed-off cartoon effects. The actors do a good enough job that they're clearly being paid, but none of them puts much more into it than that. And, in the end, there's nothing unique or interesting about it at all. I really don't understand how movies like this get made. It's not like this is somebody's dream project or has any chance of earning the producers a billion dollars. It's obviously just filler, meant to take up two hours of dead time on the Syphilis Channel or plug up a blank slot on Netflix, but there's plenty of movies like that already, even if you do limit yourself to "It has to be about Bigfoot". Was none of them available to license for less than what it cost to make this one? Movies like this are the hardest ones to review, because there's not all that much to say about them, good or bad, and even if you zing the shit out of them the people responsible will just shrug their shoulders and say "Whatever, I was just padding my resume, dude." Should I just grade it on attendance? Fine, you all showed up and, as far as I can tell, nobody dropped the camera in the river or anything, so you all pass. But with a C-. The least I can do is keep you off the dean's list.

Sasquatch: The Legend of Bigfoot

(1975)

Directed by Ed Ragozzino

In an effort to stymie future Bigfoot enthusiasts (whilst simultaneously outing poseur movie critics who don't actually watch the movies they review), there were two bullshit Bigfoot documentaries made in 1975, both called "The Legend of Bigfoot". The first one (see above) was essentially a personal labor of love and baldfaced lies centering on one guy, but this one takes a broader approach, hurling all sorts of 1970s bullshit against the wall in an effort to see what sticks. They use a stone age computer to draw a picture of Bigfoot, using "information from hundreds of sightings". (Or, you know, you could ask Rick the boom mike guy to draw it, since either way it doesn't mean fuck-all.) Indian legends about Sasquatch are dutifully trotted out, even though I strongly suspect that the Indians actually made these legends up no earlier than the 1950s, just to fuck with people. The bulk of this movie though documents a (clearly faked) expedition to find Bigfoot and tag him electronically (so that his movements and mating habits can be studied by scientists and highly specialized perverts), and once this expedition sets out it abandons all pretense that it's a documentary pretty quickly. Highlights include an absurd cougar attack (it looks like they just dropped a dead – or otherwise uncooperative – cougar onto one of the pack horses from above); an eye-rolling mountain man stereotype ("It's a *grizzly!* It's the most *ornery* animal there is!") and his semi-plausible story about Bigfoot attacking some old-school miner forty-niners; and a weak-sauce thrilling climax that is still a lot better than we've any right to expect. Oh, and of course a folksy song about Bigfoot plays over the end credits (*"High in the mountains..."*) while Bigfoot stands silently in silhouette. I half expected him to wave goodbye just before the fade-out. It's all a hilarious crock, but at least it's occasionally entertaining. Unlike, say, Animal Planet's *Finding Bigfoot*, which is just a weekly parade of overweight morons making fools of themselves. Seriously, why don't you try finding a gym, you fat fucks?

Savage

(2011)

Directed by Jordan Blum

You know, I don't care how pissed off Bigfoot gets, he's still fucking boring. In this flick he's wigging out because there's a forest fire, like he's Smokey the goddamned Bear or something. Just hide in your Bigfoot cave until it's over, asshole. But no, he has to fly off the handle and start killing people, beginning with a bunch of firemen. Which if you ask me kind of flies in the face of the point he's trying to make, but Bigfoot isn't exactly known for his brains. That why a Bigfoot has never won the Nobel Prize for his contributions to the field of anything. And he doesn't accomplish a whole lot in the course of this movie, either. He's barely even on deck for the entire first half - instead we're stuck watching this park ranger wander around bothering people and being so fucking folksy that I fully expected an arts & crafts fair to eventually fall out of his ass. I hated this jackwipe, not to mention nearly everyone else in this movie, from the annoying asshole who beats his wife, to the simpering bitch who lets him, to the tracker dude who acts like a retard's idea of a badass, right down to the "scientist" who claims that *The Lord of the Rings* turned out to be based on fact. "Tolkien was right," he declares. Okay, idiot. I'm happy to report that Bigfoot manages to kill most of these cretins before climactically exploding, but this is still a pretty lousy movie.

Shriek of the Mutilated

(1974)

Directed by Mike Findlay

Now *that's* a fucking movie title. Plus it opens with a decapitation (the head lands right in the swimming pool!) and one of our main peeps is a to-die-for redhead, who's also sporting glasses which is cinematic shorthand for "she's smart as well as hot". (So, two reasons why she would never date you.) Seriously, junior moviemakers, start taking notes. After some mysteriously-motivated domestic violence (a guy slits his girl's throat with a bread knife, but she's not quite dead so after he passes out, drunk and fully clothed, in the bathtub, she tosses a toaster in with him) we settle in to our main story, which appears to be another "search for the Yeti gone wrong" scenario until it takes a sudden left turn into complete insanity. This is one of those rare movies that doesn't waste a single scene - there's always something bizarre or ridiculous happening, whether it's a dork ad-libbing a song about the Yeti, a dismembered human leg recovered from the woods and casually left on the dining room table, dead people used as bait (*The Hills Have Yetis*), a mute played by an actor who clearly has "mute" confused with "retarded", or wonderful lines like "I wanted to hide it so you wouldn't feed it to the beast!" Some mild gore, the two main chicks are gorgeous, and even the incidental chicks are all pretty hot. I noted in the introduction that Yeti movies always seem to be better than Bigfoot movies, and this one, despite a technically that I'm not going to mention, is no exception. Full-on recommended.

The Six Million Dollar Man: "The Secret of Bigfoot"

(1976)

Written by Kenneth Johnson

If you thought about it for more than five seconds, *The Six Million Dollar Man* (or *The 25.7 Million Dollar Man*, when adjusted for inflation) was a pretty stupid program. I mean, if his arm is bionic, but the rest of his upper body isn't, wouldn't lifting something unusually heavy just tear it out of its socket? We watched it anyway though, because it was the 1970s and there wasn't a whole lot else to do except go disco dancing, and then you had to pretend you weren't super uncomfortable about all the gays. They sure could dance though. Anyway, the show ran for a while, but this is unquestionably the most famous episode, because not only does it feature the Six Million Dollar Man fighting Bigfoot, but it turns out that Bigfoot is also bionic and, just for good measure, under the control of aliens, one of whom is played by a young(ish) Stefanie "Mrs. Hart to Hart" Powers. And that's not all. There's also a tunnel of light; a Bionic Woman cameo; alien abductions; flared jumpsuits; gauzy, soft-focus photography; a Huggy Bear reference; an earthquake; and a Sasquatch-championing Injun. Seriously, we're just one musical number by Donna Summer away from summing up the entire 1970s here. You have to give them credit, though. Whereas most old TV shows would have ended with the revelation that Bigfoot is a hoax (maybe tacking on a lazy "twist" where the real Bigfoot is seen at the end, watching from the trees or something), this show careens drunkenly in the exact opposite direction. Not only is Bigfoot real, but the circumstances of his existence are ten times more fucked up then anyone could have possibly imagined without the use of hard drugs, which, perhaps not uncoincidentally, were also quite popular in the 1970s. This episode was so popular that there was even a paperback novelization of tit, because of course there was. How else could people relive the excitement in the days before VCRs? Novelizations are interesting because sometimes there's shit in them that got cut out of the actual movie or show, but the only notable differences this time are that the aliens' viewing screen is a rectangle instead of a hexagon (the book really harps on this, like a rectangular monitor is inconceivably bizarre or something), and the Six Million Dollar Man is a lot more sarcastic, repeatedly lipping off to the aliens and making several smart-assed comments that didn't appear in the show. Injecting a few smart-ass comments is a good way to pad out slight material. Or so I've heard.

The Six Million Dollar Man "The Return of Bigfoot"

(1976)

Written by Kenneth Johnson

By the end of their previous encounter the Six Million Dollar Man and Bigfoot had become regular pals (yes, it's all just as stupid as it sounds), but then the Six Million Dollar Man's memory of their entire adventure was erased, because apparently he's much luckier than the rest of us. So when Bigfoot returns and starts committing gold and emerald heists the Six Million Dollar Man is baffled, until Sandy Duncan shows up, restores his memory, and explains that some rogue, time-traveling aliens are forcing Bigfoot to help them take over the world. The Six Million Dollar Man is blamed for the heists though, and the truth is obviously too fucking retarded for anyone to swallow, so he has to go on the lam to stop them. At least that's the plan, but Bigfoot cleans his fucking clock, necessitating a crossover with *The Bionic Woman* to wrap this ludicrous shit up. It all ends with the Bionic Man, the Bionic Woman, Bionic Bigfoot, and non-bionic Sandy Duncan (I'd totally fuck her though) busting up the aliens' secret hideout while a volcano (depicted by scenes stolen from what appears to be an unrelated 1960s movie) erupts all around them. Then, to stop the flowing lava, they transport it forward in time to a point when it's already solid rock, because why the fuck not?

When it's all over, the Bionic Woman gives her new friend Bionic Bigfoot "a big, bionic hug" and that stupid bionic sound effect briefly plays, indicating either that this hug is fortified with super bionic love, or that she was actually trying to break his spine, either way makes an equal amount of sense.

Man, this show really is a lot fucking stupider than I remembered.

The Six Million Dollar Man "Bigfoot V"

(1977)

Written by Gregory S. Dinallo

Just like I can only be bothered to watch the episodes of *Knight Rider* with KARR in them, I'll only watch the episodes of this show guest-starring Bionic Bigfoot. This time Bigfoot's alien masters, good and bad, have all flown the coop, leaving him behind to crack up and go on a garden variety rampage whilst simultaneously being hassled by some chick. It's far and away the least delirious Six Million Dollar Man/Bigfoot adventure, and I'm really only including it here for the sake of completeness and also because I can't write off this *Six Million Dollar Man Season 5* box set unless I write *something* about it. Here's a question this episode did inspire though: why are people always making plaster casts of Bigfoot's footprints? What, exactly, is this supposed to prove? In fact, it suggests to me that you actually made the plaster version first, and then used that to hoax the footprints. Nice try, assholes. At any rate, at the end of the episode Bionic Bigfoot becomes a real live boy, just like fucking Pinocchio, and that's the last we ever see of him. Nigga didn't even get a cameo in the inevitable reunion movies. Still, he only appeared in five episodes and got his own action figure, trumping far more important 1970s' sci-fi icons like Apollo (*Battlestar Galactica*) and Dale Arden

(*Flash Gordon*), who appeared in every single episode of their respective shows and never got the action figure treatment at all. I suppose that counts for something.

Snowbeast

(1977)

Directed by Herb Wallerstein

This old-school TV movie is pretty tame and they barely even show the monster, but I always kinda liked it anyway. The A story concerns these ski resort jokers who get their asses handed to them by a pissed-off Yeti, but the best parts of the movie don't have anything to do with the Yeti at all. For example, at first it seems like they're gonna include some low-grade drama between these two guys who are both in love with the same bag ("I've forgotten how beautiful you are," says one of them. Yeah, it looks like she forgot too.), but then they don't even bother, like they suddenly decided (correctly) that a Yeti movie doesn't really need to be that complicated. I also liked the part where the main guy declares the Yeti attack zone off-limits ("You tell 'em to get ready to put a lot of signs up there!"), and the part where a couple escapes from a barn the Yeti's attacking and this deer skull that's hanging over the door falls off and hits the actress right in the face, for real. Then there's the weird minimalist funeral they hold for one cat in this tiny little cemetery on the side of the mountain. I know there's a cemetery exclusively for people who die climbing the Matterhorn, maybe this town has one solely for jokers who get wasted by the Snowbeast. The only thing I don't like about this flick is that the Snowbeast ultimately goes down like a total punk: all it takes to kill him in the end is some small rounds fire and a ski pole. Sounds more like the Snow*bitch* to me.

SnowBeast

(2011)

Directed by Brian Brough

I know horror movie producers were remake-happy at the time, but fucking made-for-network-TV *Snowbeast*??? At least the original *Boggy Creek* had a theatrical release. This one "improves" on the original – which featured a pretty cool-looking monster that we barely got to see – by featuring a slightly less impressive monster we see entirely too much of. Our main guy is Bo Duke, joined on the slopes by his bangable colleague (in what, I don't recall), his hot-ass attitude-prone daughter (dibs), and some negligible dork assistant (nice hair, queer) who's destined to die in order to drum up some cheap pathos, because there's no way they'll kill any of the other three. There's a painful, hilariously forced father-daughter bonding moment over a lynx; the scenes where the monster jogs in circles around people, undetected, are astronomically retarded; and, astoundingly, I was finally wrong about something: the monster does kill the romantic interest/colleague, and it kills her pretty good, too. Oh, and there's no pathos at all when the assistant gets it. His companions just abandon that sap to die. Ultimately, this is, at best, another average, also-ran monster movie, just like the original. Way to aim low, junior achievers.

The Snow Creature

(1954)

Directed by W. Lee Wilder

It's like s'no creature you know! Ha ha ha ha ha ha ha! Yeah. So, this scientific expedition is hoofing it into the Himalayas to study the local foliage. (That's plants, and if you're thinking that there really can't be that many interesting plants growing in a frozen, mountainous region like the Himalayas I'd agree with you. But the main cat in the 1957 movie *The Abominable Snowman* was doing the same thing, so maybe it was one of those 1950s fads, like the hula hoop or listening to race music.) When a ratty-looking Yeti snatches one of the local women though, our main guy comes up with a new plan: track that rapey fucker down and rescue her. Ha ha! I am *totally* kidding. Actually, he's highly irritated that the Sherpas want to mount a rescue mission, never mind that the woman in question is his guide's *wife*. He goes so far as to threaten to shoot anyone who inconveniences him by going after her, and in the end he only agrees "help" (by which I mean not actively hinder) the rescue operation after the Sherpas relieve him of all his ammo and his guide shoots their radio. When they finally track the Yeti down to its cave it starts flailing around like a spazmo, bringing the whole place down on itself, and during the confusion our main guy gets his gun back, takes the Yeti captive, and marches everyone back down the mountain at gunpoint, leaving the guide's wife to her fate. Once back in town he has everyone arrested, then makes a show of not pressing charges so he can enjoy watching the guide grovel thankfully at his feet. Karma catches up to him when he ships the Yeti back to the 'States though - it's immediately seized by the government because of the its undefined immigration status! Ha ha ha ha! (Dear Makers of *The Snow Creature*: red tape is an incredibly boring plot complication, by the way.) Of course the Yeti eventually escapes and goes on a laughable rampage, and of course our main guy is more concerned with re-capturing it alive than how many innocent people it kills. I want to stress here that at no time is our main cat portrayed as the bad guy; he is legitimately and unironically the acknowledged hero of this story, making everything he does a jaw-dropping laugh riot. Too bad that's pretty much all this flick has going for it. I did like the fight this couple is having in the street right before the Yeti shows up ("I'm sick of listening to your words!"), but the monster action is a fucking joke, and it's not like there's anybody to root for since the only character we follow from beginning to end is a raging dick. This flick is usually identified as the first ever Bigfoot/Yeti movie, but a Finnish movie called *Pete and Runt on the Trail of the Abominable Snowman* (starring the Finnish Abbott & Costello) (because such a thing exists, apparently) came out the very same year, so in the end it doesn't even have that to distinguish it. And I'm glad, because this movie doesn't deserve any distinction, even of the incidental variety. It's a piece of crap.

The Snow Devils

(1965)

Directed by Anthony Dawson

Well it turns out kicking the catalytic converter off my car wasn't the cause of global warming after all - it's actually alien Abominable Snowmen (sporting green leotards and pimp-ass gold medallions) who want to flood the planet! It's a fucking space emergency and only one cat can handle the job, but, wouldn't you know it, he's on leave! Space Command checks all his usual haunts – playing Putt-Putt with a babe in a bikini, hanging out at the gym with a Japanese stereotype ("I'm so sorry. Commander reft an hour ago.") – and finally they track him down playing checkers against some little kid (and losing, I might add). Once he's briefed on the situation stat he locates the Snowmen's base and trashes it, but it turns out they have a second one located in outer space and naturally it's a race against time to find it before the entire world is turned into beachfront property. It sounds pretty wild so it's too bad almost nothing actually happens in this flick - most of the time everyone's just sitting around running data or telling someone else to engage the "eon drive" (I think they meant "ion drive", but who the hell knows with these clowns). At the very end they drop a bunch of asteroids on the snowmen, which is relatively hilarious, but the rest of this Italian hack job is just a boring, lame-ass pizza shit.

Stomp! Shout! Scream!

(2005)

Directed by Jay Wade Edwards

This is another one of those goddamn fucking flicks that dresses up like a much older movie but doesn't have any funny or interesting observations that make it better than just watching an old movie in the first place. I am seriously over this shit - it's like the movie equivalent of tracing. The setup is basically "Chick Band vs. Skunk Ape", and if those words don't make any sense to you in that order then you're probably not from Florida, because any Floridian worth her permanently sun-damaged skin knows that the Skunk Ape is a mysterious creature that's the missing link between skunk and ape. Or something like that. Usually dropping a chick band into a lousy a movie means that at least there's *something* to look at, but not this time because two of the bandtwats are dumpster-ugly and the third one (the drummer), who's actually worth a sticking, never takes her clothes off. In fact, no girls get naked in this movie, which might be okay if it was gory, funny, interesting, or just didn't exist at all, but it doesn't have any of those things going for it so the only reason for you to watch is if you're some sort of Skunk Ape completist, in which case this DVD is probably already sitting on your shelf right next to the only other Skunk Ape movie I can think of, *Erin Brockovich*.

Strange Wilderness

(2008)

Directed by Fred Wolf

Did you ever see the 2006 movie *Grandma's Boy*? It has no plot whatsoever, and almost all the jokes revolve around smoking pot, old people doing and saying outrageous/unexpected things, and a monkey. It should be terrible, but against all odds it's one of the funniest movies around. Well this flick is from the same people (Well some of them, anyway. Do I look like I have time to read every single movie credit? I'm not on the committee that selects Oscar nominees, you know.), but I guess they all stopped caring or were really depressed by 2008 because *Strange Wilderness* is about as funny as *I Spit on Your Grave*. Living it, I mean, not watching it.

This wildlife show is about to be canceled due to gross incompetence, so the guys behind it decide that their only chance to boost the ratings is for them to prove the existence of Bigfoot. (I'd like to point out that a previous episode of their show that we see has topless chicks in it, and if that didn't boost the ratings I highly doubt Bigfoot will. Nevertheless, that's the premise of this movie and we're stuck with it.) Along the way the main guy gets his dick stuck in a turkey's throat, one cat repeatedly takes a joy buzzer to the dick, and they all make fun of their guide because his name is Dick. There's some really broad comedy, too. (Seriously though, this flick is so obsessed with dick that it almost counts as gay porn. Look, guys who made this movie, just because girls laugh when they see *your* dick doesn't mean that all dicks are automatically hilarious, okay?) There are a few legitimately funny bits (they cook and eat several piranha to get petty revenge on the piranha for eating their friend; "We're in the middle of a fucking conversation and you turn around to hit on some chick?"), but overall it's pretty forgettable. Bigfoot appears on screen for like 30 seconds.

Suburban Sasquatch

(2004)

Directed by Dave Wascavage

Welp, it seems Sasquatch has had enough (I can certainly relate), and he's one cat who doesn't need to wait three days for a background check before going on a homicidal rampage. First to go: a hopeless dork and his cute... Christ, I hope that's his sister. From there Sasquatch rips one fisherdude's arm off and throws it at a second fisherdude, knocking the latter out; slaps and then drags off a single mom right in front of her kid (we've all been there, right?); dismembers two cute hikers (one of them grows her torn-off arm back after she dies, but Sasquatch just pulls it off again and then eats her, clothes and all); tears a small dog to pieces and crushes its owner's chest; and so on. It's worse than you think though, because this Sasquatch has the power to teleport... or turn invisible... or something (also, I think he's riding a skateboard in at least one scene), and as a consequence the only one who can take him out is this typically mystical Indian chick (casino, not 7-11) who is so spit-takingly hot that you will probably question reality when you see her. I'm not kidding; there is nothing, *nothing,* I wouldn't do for a crack at this chick, including taking it from behind by Sasquatch first. She makes this entire movie, nay, the existence of the universe, worthwhile. Too bad she never gets naked. In fact, the only nippage on hand is the Sasquatch's, and those are plastic, prompting several unfortunate flashbacks to George Clooney's Batman. This flick is irrefutably backyard cinema at its backyardiest: the monster's just a cheap-ass suit, the regular effects are dodgy at best, and the cartoon effects are the worst imaginable. (Seriously, whoever did these cartoon effects should have his legal right to own a computer revoked, like those kids who hack into government websites and shit.) If you're willing to meet it on those terms, though, it's fairly entertaining. Best line:

MOM: "Monsters are not real - like the boogeyman or your Father, they're not really there."

Terror in the Midnight Sun

(1959)

Directed by Virgil Vogel

Holy shit, Lapland is a real place??? I though it was a idiom or whatever, you know, like "Hey, baby, why don't you wiggle that ass on over here and visit Lapland?" Well anyway, a meteor has crashed there, but this is a science fiction movie so of course it's not really a meteor, it's a UFO. Much dicking around commences, until finally the aliens unleash their secret weapon: a gigantic Bigfoot! (To put his size in perspective for you, he's not quite as big as Mighty Joe Young, but at least a little bigger than Shaq. At one point, though, he's closer to classic King Kong size. I'm not sure if this is because he ate all his Star Wheaties right before this scene, or the aliens souped him up a bit, or the moviemakers were just that incompetent, or what. But it's probably the latter.) Space Bigfoot busts some shit up, kills several reindeer (Blitzen, no!), and, naturally, carries off the main chick at one point. (And this chick, let me tell you: she is beyond aces. I would fuck her all over the map. This movie's way too short to waste so much time on the main guy trying to land her though. Seal the deal already, Casanova, we haven't got all day.) In the end a torch-wielding mob (it can't be easy to wield torches when you're on skis, but somehow they manage) chases Space Bigfoot down, sets him on fire, and he falls off a cliff, after which his alien masters, understandably, slink off in embarrassment. The theme song that plays over the end credits is called "Midnight Sun Lament". Seems appropriate. Not a great movie by any recognized standard, but I suppose it's passable. Of course, so are kidney stones.

The Untold

(2002)

Directed by Jonas Quastel

A plane has crashed, and various interested parties are fucking off into the semi-accessible wilderness area where it went down to see if they can locate it. "Alright, cut the chatter, people!" demands one cat as they set out. Why? This isn't a military operation. Don't be such a controlling asshole, dude. Unfortunately, they'd all be better off if this *were* a military operation, because there's a Sasquatch out there, a Sasquatch that can see heat like the Predator, has bulletproof skin, and is smart enough to understand DNA testing and shit. It's a goddamned CSI Supersquatch. You might think that the aforementioned would be plenty of stupid for one tossed-off Bigfoot flick, but these moviemakers sure didn't. Case in point: for some inexplicable reason they decided that the picture should be constantly fading to black and back, not just between scenes but right in the middle of scenes too. At one point it happens *four times* during one (short) conversation! I suppose some idiot thought that this looked "extreme" or "kewl" or "RTFM" or something, but the overall effect is similar to when you're watching a movie so boring that you can barely keep your eyes open, which turns out to be pretty appropriate. No real gore, one pair of stunt tits, and, *yet again,* featuring the cat from *Pumpkinhead* and *Millennium.* How many fucking

Bigfoot movies is he in, anyway? Do the producers think that his presence somehow makes these movies seem less low-rent and crappy? Because it doesn't.

The Wild Man of the Navidad

(2008)

Directed by Duane "Sissy Boy" Graves and Justin "I'm a Little Girl in Pigtails and a Pink Dress" Meeks

The *Wild Man of the Navidad* DVD opens with some cornhead telling us how "scary" and "dangerous" the two guys who made this movie are, over footage of said guys shooting old cans with a handgun. This, of course, immediately pegs them as detestable pussies, who just made my "bitch-slap on sight" list. If it ever happens (and please let it), they'll break down crying on the spot, I guarantee it. As for the movie itself, it's definitely not what I was hoping for (the long-awaited Christmas-themed Bigfoot horror/gore movie), but if nothing else props to this 2008 flick for trying its best to look like something that was actually made in the late 1970s/early 1980s, approximately the last time anyone took Bigfoot even remotely seriously. Hell, they even found an old pull-tab beer can for someone to open during the bar scene. Remember those? Instead of popping the can open, the entire tab peeled off, resulting in a sharp, curly little piece of metal that you just tossed aside for someone to step on or an endangered turtle to eat or whatever. They were great. Anyway, the story, which claims to be true (whatever), concerns cinema's least impressive trio – a pathetic, unemployed hick; his ugly, paralyzed wife;

and the shirtless, panty-sniffing redneck who lives with them – and the trouble they get... excuse me... *git* into when they lease out some land that's already been claimed by Bigfoot. That's right, it's basically a movie about a landlord/tenant dispute, except the tenant is Bigfoot and instead of putting his rent in escrow he brutally slaughters everyone. Now, our main dude knows what's happening, but he needs the money so he just keeps right on sending lessees to their doom (there's a whole "sending people to their Bigfoot-induced death" montage, in fact; naturally, country music plays over this part) until Bigfoot mercilessly eviscerates the town's sole hottie and everyone has finally had enough, at which point the racist sheriff rounds up every beardo, drunk, yokel, and fatass he can find and they run Bigfoot to ground. The actual Bigfoot monster looks like he's made out of old bags, there's a *Brimstone & Treacle*-flavored sideplot that exists solely to make us puke, and of course the story is total shit because let's face it, when your "based on a true story" is about something that everyone knows doesn't exist, you've pretty much written yourself into a corner before you've even begun.

An awful, awful movie. Directed by pussies.

Willow Creek

(2013)

Directed by Bobcat Goldthwait

I suppose Bigfoot movies do lend themselves particularly well to the lost & found footage treatment, but that doesn't mean I have to like it. The real question is: How did something this terrible come from the same guy who gave us the beyond-genius classic *Shakes the Clown* (1991)? I mean, did he have a stroke in the interim or something? Two annoying tools (imagine the most irritating couple you know, and multiply that x 2) with a videocamera traipse off into the woods looking for Bigfoot, where they're eventually killed (and almost certainly eaten) by what a skillful freeze-frame reveals to be a morbidly obese fat chick. Frankly, the world is better off without them. It's massively padded even at 79 minutes, it's boring (at one point, out main couple sits in a tent and stares at the camera for a solid *ten minutes* of real time while nothing happens), and it's shot lost & found footage style so it's not a real movie anyway. Fuck this piece of fucking shit. Fuck it raw and then abort its idiot child. It's a fucking disgrace.

The Woodsman

(2012)

Directed by Christian Cisneros

More lost & found footage garbage, which I'm including here solely to remind everyone that lost & found footage deals are *not* real movies and can *always* be dismissed offhand, since the only prerequisites for "making" one are a) owning a camera (or even a goddamned *phone*) and b) having no shame. Seriously, how can anyone make one of these with a straight face anymore? I sat through every frame of *The Woodsman* though, because it's my job, and as you probably guessed it's "about" a guy wandering around in the woods with a camera until ~~the Blair Witch~~ Bigfoot gets him. (The in-story reason for his being out there is that he's shooting footage for a reality show, although based on what we see here it's a show almost as pointless and shitty as this movie.) And you should see him cry after he finds his friend half-eaten by Bigfoot! Man up, pussy. *The Woodsman* is boring, it's lazy, the main guy is an annoying dilmarker, it's not a real movie, Christian Cisneros is a "director" in the same way that driving to 7-ll for cigarettes makes you Dale Earnhardt, Apple products are overrated, traffic around here is terrible, teachers and nurses get paid plenty, and Walmart's everyday low prices are completely canceled out by their even-more-often-a-day shitty service. "To all those of you, out there watching this, I want to apologize," says the main guy at the end. Apology not accepted. Fuck *The Woodman*, and fuck lost & found footage in general. I'm so tired of this minimal-effort-expended bullshit.

Yeti

(2008)

Directed by Paul Ziller

A plane full of football players crashes in the mountains, but before they can start eating each other, a Yeti does it for them. Football players, huh? Alright, you've got sixty seconds to give me one good reason why we shouldn't root for the Yeti.

Time. Okay, that said this flick isn't too bad. Basically all they did was take that old cannibal rugby team flick *Survive!* (1976) and throw in a Yeti, but there are worse ideas for a movie and this does have some cool shit in it, like a guy using his dead buddy's arm for a splint, dumb jocks finally serving a purpose (lunch), and some hilarious Yeti-on-idiots violence. Another plus is the actual Yeti: yes, it's a little goofy-looking, but at least it's not a goddamned cartoon the whole time. (It is sometimes though, and of course then it looks utterly retarded, especially when it's jumping around like the Incredible Hulk.) On the half empty side, I was super pissed that the chink bitch survived, because seriously, what an epic cunt. The Yeti was leaving all the survivors alone because there were already plenty of dead bodies for it to chow on, so what does this twat do? She burns them! And as if that isn't bad enough, those bodies were all the survivors had for food too! Me, I would've caved her worthless skull in on the spot. We could've eaten Chinese for a week. (Insert your own "hungry again an hour later" joke here.)

I also could've done without the ridiculous Sylvester Stallone in *Cliffhanger* ending with the Yeti hanging from a guy who's hanging from a branch that's hanging over a cliff. So this movie isn't perfect, but ultimately the missteps are a small price to pay to see a Yeti deliver a rib shot to a guy with said guy's own severed leg.

Don't miss out!

Visit the website below and you can sign up to receive emails whenever Mr. Satanism publishes a new book. There's no charge and no obligation.

https://books2read.com/r/B-A-TCXC-WCXP

BOOKS 2 READ

Connecting independent readers to independent writers.

Also by Mr. Satanism

66.6 Absurd Movies About the Devil
Legendary House of Haunted Hell
Trash of the Titans
Night of the Living Dud
Lifetime Movies... for Men
Shark Weak: The Worst Shark Movies Ever Made
The Not-At-All-Cleverly-Titled Book of Dragon Movies
Snakes, Rats, Spiders, and Bats: A Creepy-Crawly Movie
Compendium
Monkeys & Dinosaurs: Cinema as High Art, Vol. 1
Hex Crimes: The Worst Witch Movies Ever Made
Close Encounters of the Worst Kind
Triskaidekaphilia - Mr. Satanism's 13th Book
Vampire Movies Suck
Werewolves Don't Eat Brunch
Mr. Satanism's Invisible Book
A Yeti Brew (And Bigfoot Too)
The Magical Golden Rainbow Book of Crappy Wizard of Oz
Movies
Cannibal Attraction
A Chronology on Elm Street
Mr. Satanism Puts Down Your Favorite Dog (...Movies)
A Collection of Woke Movie Reviews

www.ingramcontent.com/pod-product-compliance
Lightning Source LLC
Chambersburg PA
CBHW071338130726
47996CB00002B/783